The Anti-Racism Resource Guide

Volume One:

Supporting Black Businesses and Economics©

Kirk A. Johnson

Cherish Blackness.

Table of Contents

Black Owned Banks	1
Publicly Traded Black Owned Banks, Companies & Racial Equity ETF	2
Black Owned Credit Unions	3
Black Owned Financial Services for Personal/Corporate Investments & Advisement	4
Black Owned Real Estate & Construction Companies	6
Black Owned Technology Companies	7
General Black Business Funding & Programs	8
Funding & Resources for Black Women Entrepreneurs	10
Black Owned Online Directories, Resources	11
Black Owned E-commerce & Supermarkets-Food Products	12
Black Owned Health Products & Resources	16
Black Owned Farms	18
Black Owned Personal Products	21
Black Owned Household Goods	30
Black Owned Cleaning & Design Services	32
Black Owned Apparel Companies	33
Black Owned Kid, Games & Toy Companies	39
Racial Justice Initiatives	41

BLACK-OWNED ECONOMICS

Black Owned Banks

Alamerica Bank
2170 Highland Avenue
Birmingham, AL 35205
(205) 558-4600
https://www.alamericabank.com

Broadway Federal Bank (Merged with City First Bank)
5055 Wilshire Boulevard, Suite 100
Los Angeles, CA 90036
(323) 931-1886
https://www.broadwayfederalbank.com

Carver Federal Savings
1825 Park Avenue
New York, NY 10035
(718) 230-2900
https://www.carverbank.com

Carver State Bank
701 Martin Luther King, Jr. Boulevard
Savannah, Georgia 31415
(877) 489-2434
https://www.carverstatebank.com

Citizens Savings Bank & Trust
2013 Jefferson Street
Nashville, TN 37208
https://www.bankcbn.com
(615) 327-9787

Citizens Trust Bank
965 Martin Luther King Jr. Drive
Atlanta, GA, 30314
(678) 406-4000
https://ctbconnect.com
State Locations: GA, AL

Columbia Savings & Loan
2020 W Fond Du Lac Avenue
Milwaukee, WI 53205
(414) 374-0486
https://www.columbiasavingsandloans.com

Commonwealth National Bank
2214 St. Stephens Road
Mobile, AL 36617
(251) 476-5938
https://www.ecommonwealthbank.com

First Independence Bank
7310 Woodward Ave., Ste. 101
Detroit, MI 48202
(313) 256-8400
https://www.firstindependence.com

GN Bank (Illinois Service Federal Bank)
4619 S King Dr
Chicago, IL 60653
(773) 624-2000
https://www.gnbank.net

Harbor Bank of Maryland
25 West Fayette Street
Baltimore, Maryland 21201
(888) 833-7920
https://www.theharborbank.com

Industrial Bank (acquired City National Bank of New Jersey)
4812 Georgia Avenue N.W.
Washington, D.C. 20011
(202) 722-2000 [phone]
(800) 461-5056 [after hours]
https://www.industrial-bank.com
State Locations: DC, MD, NJ, NY

Liberty Bank (Acquired Metro Bank, KY)
2714 Canal Street
New Orleans, LA 70119
(800) 883-3943
https://www.libertybank.net
State Locations: LA, MI, IL, MS, KS, MO, KY, AL

Mechanics & Farmers Bank (M&F Bank)
2705 Durham-Chapel Hill Boulevard
Durham, North Carolina
(919) 687-7811
https://www.mfbonline.com

One United Bank
3683 Crenshaw Boulevard
Los Angeles, CA 90016
Phone: (877) 663-8648
https://www.oneunited.com
State Locations: CA, FL, MA

Optus Bank (formerly South Carolina Community Bank)
1545 Sumter Street
Columbia, SC 29201
(803) 733-8100
https://www.optus.bank

Tri-State Bank of Memphis
4606 Elvis Presley Boulevard
Memphis, TN 38116
(901) 398-1342
https://www.tristatebank.com

United Bank of Philadelphia
30 South 15th Street, 1st Floor
Philadelphia, PA 19102
(215) 231-3674
https://www.ubphila.com

Unity National Bank of Houston
2602 Blodgett Street
Houston, TX 77004
(713) 387-7400
https://www.unitybanktexas.com
State Locations: TX, GA

Publicly Traded Black Owned Banks, Companies & Racial Equity ETF

DISCLAIMER: Before using financial services and investing always consult with a financial professional.

American Shared Hospital Services (AMS)
http://www.ashs.com

Axsome Therapeutics (AXSM)
http://www.axsome.com

Broadway Financial (BYFC)
http://www.broadwayfederalbank.com

Carver Bancorp (CARV)
http://www.carverbank.com

Citizens Bancshares Georgia (CZBS)
http://www.ctbconnect.com

Impact Shares NAACP Minority Empowerment ETF (NACP)

Industrial Bank (IBWC)
http://www.industrial-bank.com

Jumia Technologies AG (JMIA)
http://group.jumia.com

M&F Bancorp (MFBP)
http://www.mfbonline.com

RLJ Lodging (RLJ)
http://www.rljlodgingtrust.com

The Dream Exchange (First Black Owned Stock Exchange)
https://dreamex.com

Urban One (UONE, UONEK)
http://www.urban1.com

Black Owned Credit Unions

1st Choice Credit Union
315 Auburn Avenue
Atlanta, GA 30303
(404) 832-5800
https://1stchoicecu.org

Brookland Federal Credit Union
949 Sunset Boulevard
West Columbia, SC 29169
(803) 794-9201
https://www.brooklandfcu.org

Community Owned Federal Credit Union
117 Spring Street #C,
Charleston, SC 29403
Phone: (843) 722-7656
https://cofederalcreditunion.com

Credit Union of Atlanta
670 Metropolitan Parkway SW
Atlanta, GA 30310
(404) 658-6465
https://www.cuatlanta.org

Faith Community United Credit Union
3550 East 93rd Street (near 93rd and Union)
Cleveland, Ohio 44105-1644
(216) 271-7111
http://www.faithcommcu.com

Faith Cooperative Federal Credit Union
2020 West Wheatland Road
Dallas, Texas 75232
(972) 228-5222
http://www.faithcfcu.com

FAMU Federal Credit Union
1610 South Monroe Street
Tallahassee, FL 32301
(850) 222-4541
https://famufcu.com

First Legacy Community Credit Union
431 Beatties Ford Road
Charlotte, North Carolina 28216
(704) 375-5781
https://www.firstlegacyccu.org

Greater Kinston Credit Union
901 N. Queen Street
Kinston, NC 28501
(252) 527-4002
https://www.greaterkcu.org

Hill District Federal Credit Union
2021 Centre Avenue
Pittsburgh, PA 15219
(412) 281-0822
https://www.hilldistrictfcu.org

Hope Federal Credit Union
4 Old River Place, Suite A
Jackson, MS 39202
(866) 321-4673
https://hopecu.org
State Locations: AL, AR, LA, MS, TN

Mount Olive Baptist Church
Federal Credit Union
514 N. L. Robinson Drive
Arlington, TX 76011
(817) 261-9325
http://www.mobcfcu.com

Oak Cliff Christian FCU
1130 W. Camp Wisdom Road
Dallas, TX 75232
(214) 672-9180
http://occfcu.org

Omega Psi Phi Fraternity Federal Credit Union
c/o CAMO
568 Liberty Hill Road
Toccoa, GA 30577-7996
(800) 426-6342
https://oppffcu.com

South Side Community Federal Credit Union
5401 S. Wentworth Avenue, #25 Suite 19E
Chicago, IL 60609
(773) 548-5500
http://www.southsidecommunityfcu.org

Southern Teachers & Parents
Federal Credit Union
728 Harding Boulevard
Baton Rouge, LA 70807
(225) 775-8597
https://www.stpfcu.com

St. Louis Community Credit Union
3651 Fores Park Avenue
St. Louis, MO 63108
(314) 534-7610
https://www.stlouiscommunity.com

Toledo Urban Federal Credit Union
1441 Dorr Street
Toledo, Ohio 43607
(419) 255.8876
https://www.toledourban.net

Black Owned Financial Services for Personal/Corporate Investments & Advisement

Advent Capital Management L.L.C.
888 Seventh Avenue, 31st Floor
New York, NY 10019
(212) 482 1600
https://www.adventcap.com

Ariel Investments
c/o U.S. Bank Global Fund Services
P.O. Box 701
Milwaukee, WI 53201-0701
(800) 292-7435
https://www.arielinvestments.com

Awoye Capital
1000 Woodbury Road, Suite 300
Woodbury, NY 11797
(516) 358-3738
http://www.awoyecapital.com

Blaylock Van, LLC
600 Lexington Ave
3rd Floor
New York, NY, 10022
(212) 715-6600
https://brv-llc.com

Blueprint Capital Advisors
45 Academy Street, Suite 205
Newark, NJ 07102
(212) 390-1155
https://blueprintllc.com

Brown Capital Management
1201 North Calvert Street
Baltimore, MD 21202
(877) 892-4226
https://browncapital.com

Capri Capital Partners LLC
875 N Michigan Avenue #3430
Chicago, IL 60611
(312) 573-5300
https://capri.global

Cadiz Capital Holdings
1203 Jimson Circle SE– Suite 501
Atlanta, GA 30013
(314) 409-6918
https://www.cadizcapital.com

Castle Oak Securities LP
110 E 59th Street #5
New York, NY 10022
(646) 521-6700
http://www.castleoaklp.com

Channing Capital Management, LLC
10 S LaSalle Street #2401
Chicago, IL 60603
(312) 223-0211
https://www.channingcapital.com

Data Gration Consulting Group
https://www.data-gration.com

Delancey Wealth Management
20 F Street NW

Washington, DC 20001
(202) 507-6340
https://www.delanceywealth.com

Edgar Lomax Company
The Edgar Lomax Company
5971 Kingstowne Village Parkway Suite 240
Alexandria, VA 22315
(703) 719-0026
https://www.edgarlomax.com

Fairview Capital Partners Inc.
75 Isham Road, Suite 200
West Hartford, CT 06107
(860) 674-8066
http://fairviewcapital.com
State Locations: CT, CA

Fola Financial
https://www.folafinancial.com

GenNx360 Capital Partners
590 Madison Avenue
New York, NY 10022
(212) 257-6790
http://gennx360.com

Golden Door Asset Management
https://www.goldendoorasset.com

Grain Management L.L.C.
19 West 44th Street Suite 1702
New York, NY 10036
(929) 506-5900
https://www.graingp.com
State Locations: NY, DC, FL

ICV Partners L.L.C.
810 7th Avenue 35th Floor
New York, NY 10019
(212) 455-9600
https://www.icvpartners.com
State Locations: NY, GA

Loop Capital

111 W. Jackson Boulevard
Suite 1901
Chicago, IL 60604
(312) 913-4900
https://www.loopcapital.com

Muller & Monroe Asset Management
180 N Stetson Avenue #1320
Chicago, IL 60601
(312) 782-7771
https://www.m2am.com

NPM Accounting & Advisory, LLC
202 N 15th Street
Bloomfield, NJ, 07003
(862) 757-8559
https://npmadvisory.com

Pharos Capital Group L.L.C.
112 Enfield Road
Baltimore, MD 21212
(410) 323-1105
https://www.pharosfunds.com
State Locations: MD, TX, TN

Powell Capital Markets Inc.
3 Becker Farm Road
Roseland, NJ 07068
(973) 740-1230
http://www.powellcapital.com

Progress Investment Management Company
33 New Montgomery Street, 19th Floor
San Franciso, CA 94105
(415) 512 3480
https://www.progressinvestment.com

Pugh Capital Management Inc
520 Pike Street
Seattle, WA 98101
(206) 322-4985
https://www.pughcapital.com

Semper Capital Management L.P.
52 Vanderbilt Avenue #401
New York, NY 10017
(212) 612-9000

http://sempercap.com

Siebert Williams Shank & Company
100 Wall Street, 18th Floor
New York, NY 10005
(646) 775-4850
https://siebertwilliams.com
State Locations: NY, CA, GA, MA, IL, MI, FL, PA, RI, MO, DC, CT, TX, HI, WA

Smith, Graham & Co. Investment Advisors L.P.
140 Broadway #4510
New York, NY 10005
(212) 487-5100
https://smithgraham.com

Stanfield Global
11140 Rockville Pike #400
Rockville, MD 20852
(301) 232-3625
https://www.stanfield.global

Stone Ridge Investment Partners
201 King of Prussia Road Suite 200
Radnor, PA 19087
(484) 254-5400
https://stoneridgeinvestments.com

Vista Equity Partners
401 Congress Avenue
Suite 3100
Austin, TX 78701
(512) 730-2400
https://www.vistaequitypartners.com
State Locations: TX, IL, NY, CA

Black Owned Real Estate & Construction Companies

Brown & Momen
823 E Drexel Square
Chicago, IL 60615
(773) 493-3743
http://brownmomen.com

C.D. Moody Construction Company
6017 Redan Road
Lithonia, GA 30058
(770) 482-7778
https://cdmoodyconstruction.com

Coleman Construction
(323) 295-5484
http://www.colemancon.com

Emmitt Smith Enterprise
14902 Preston Road
Suite 404-1042
Dallas, TX 75254
(972) 674-3124
https://www.esmithlegacy.com

ENVIRO AgScience
1190 Buckner Road
Columbia, SC 49203-4416
(803) 714-7290
http://enviroags.com

H.J. Russell & Company
171 17th St NW #1600
Atlanta, GA 30363
(404) 330-1000
https://www.hjrussell.com

Integrated Capital
11150 Santa Monica Boulevard, Suite 1680
Los Angeles, CA 90025
(310) 575-8801
http://www.intcapllc.com

MacFarlane Partners
201 Spear Street, Suite 1000
San Francisco, CA 94105
(415) 356-2500
https://www.macfarlanepartners.com

McKissack & McKissack
901 K Street, NW 6th Floor
Washington, DC 20001
(202) 347-1446
https://www.mckinc.com

MZM Construction & Management Company
105 Lock Street, Suite 205
Newark, NJ 07103
(973) 242-7100
http://mzmcc.com

Nukak Development
714 N. Massachusetts Avenue
Lakeland, Florida 33801
(863) 686-1565
http://nujak.com

Omni New York
909 3rd Avenue 21st floor
New York, NY 10022
(646) 502-7200
http://www.onyllc.com

Powers & Sons Construction Company
5040 South State Street
Chicago, IL 60609
(773) 536-3100
http://powersandsons.com

RLJ Development
https://www.rljcompanies.com/companies/rlj-financial

Safeway Construction Company
4327 W. Roosevelt Road
Chicago, Illinois 60624
(773) 522-3000
www.safewayconstruction.com

Salamander Hotels & Resorts
https://www.salamanderhotels.com

SLR Contracting & Service Company
260 Michigan Ave # 1
Buffalo, NY 14203
(716) 896-8148

Sweeten (Contractor & Construction Finder)
https://sweeten.com

The Peebles Corporation
50 West Street, 3rd Floor
Entrance on Washington Street
New York, NY 10006
(212) 355-1655
http://www.peeblescorp.com

UJAMAA Construction
7744 S Stony Island Avenue
Chicago, IL 60649
(773) 374-1300
https://ujamaaconstruction.com

Black Owned Technology Companies

4D Healthware
https://www.4dhealthware.com

AbiliLife
https://www.abililife.com

Airfordable
https://www.airfordable.com

Andela
https://andela.com

Black Girls Code
https://www.blackgirlscode.com

BREAUX Capital
https://www.breauxcapital.com

Calendly
https://calendly.com

Capway
https://www.capway.co

Diversant (IT Staffing)
https://www.diversant.com

EnrichHer
https://enrichher.com

Esusu
https://esusurent.com

Global Commerce & Services
https://www.globalcommserv.com

GoalSetter
https://www.goalsetter.co

Incluzion
https://incluzion.co

Innclusive
http://www.innclusive.com

Invest Sou Sou
https://investsousou.com

Jamborow
https://jamborow.com

Johnson Battery Technologies
https://www.johnsonbatterytech.com

JOURNi
http://www.journi.org

Kiverdi
https://www.kiverdi.com

LISNR
https://lisnr.com

Mahmee
https://www.mahmee.com

Noirbnb
https://noirbnb.com

OnceLogix
http://oncelogix.com

Ovamba Solutions
https://www.ovamba.com

Pindrop
https://www.pindrop.com

PopCom
https://www.popcom.shop

PopSocial
https://popsocial.com

Qoins
https://qoins.io

Ralph Walker Designs
https://www.ralphwalkerdesigns.com

Rapier Solutions
https://rapiersolutions.com

Raycon
https://rayconglobal.com

Rubitection
http://rubitection.com

Shine App (Anxiety & Depression)
https://join.shinetext.com

SpenDebt
https://spendebt.com

Valence Community
https://www.valence.community

Walker and Company
https://walkerandcompany.com

WeSolar
http://wesolar.energy

Zume
https://zume.com

General Black Business Funding & Programs

1863 Ventures
https://1863ventures.net

Accion U.S. Network
https://us.accion.org

Association for Enterprise Opportunity
(Partnership with Paypal)

https://aeoworks.org/paypalgrant

Backstage Capital
https://backstagecapital.com

Black Business Association

Black Enterprise Elevator Pitch Competition
www.blackenterprise.com/entrepreneurssummit/elevator-pitch

BLK Projek
http://theblkprojek.org

Cake Ventures
https://www.cake.vc

Cleo Capital
https://www.cleocap.com

Coalition of Black Trade Unionist
1155 Connecticut Avenue Suite 500
Washington, DC 20036
(202) 778-3318
https://www.cbtu.org

Collab Capital
384 Northyards Boulevard NW, Suite 100
Atlanta, GA 30313
invest@collab.capital
https://collab.capital

Community Development Financial Institutions Fund
https://www.cdfifund.gov

Disadvantaged Business Enterprise Program
https://www.transportation.gov/civil-rights/disadvantaged-business-enterprise

Empowerment Network
2401 Lake Street, Suite 110
Omaha, NE 68111
(402) 502-5153
https://empoweromaha.com

Expanding Black Business Credit Initiative
https://ebbcfund.org

Fearless Fund
https://www.fearless.fund

Fedex Small Business Grant Contest
http://smallbusinessgrant.fedex.com

GE Ventures
https://www.ge.com/licensing

Google for Startups Accelerator
Black Founders
https://events.withgoogle.com/google-for-startups-accelerator-black-founders/#content

Grants.gov Program Management Office
www.grants.gov/web/grants/home.html

Growing Power (Farming)
https://growingpower.co.uk

Hello Alice
https://blackbiz.helloalice.com

Impact America Fund
https://www.impactamericafund.com

Kapor Capital
https://www.kaporcapital.com

LISC Small Business Relief Grants
https://www.lisc.org

Marcy Venture Partners
https://www.marcyvp.com

Minority Business Development Agency (MBDA) Business Grants
www.MBDA.gov/main/grantcompetitions (grant competitions)
www.MBDA.gov/businesscenters (minority business centers)

MORTAR
https://wearemortar.com

National Association for the Self Employed (NASE) Growth Grants
www.nase.org/Membership/GrantsandScholarships/BusinessDevelopmentGrants.aspx

National Association of Black Accountants, Inc
7474 Greenway Center Drive, Suite 1120
Greenbelt, Maryland 20770
(301) 474-6222
https://www.nabainc.org

National Association of Real Estate Brokers
9831 Greenbelt Road
lanham, MD, 20706
(301) 552-9340
http://www.nareb.com

National Black MBA Association (NBMBAA) Scale-Up Pitch Challenge
www.nbmbaa.org/scale-up-pitch-challenge

National Black McDonald's Operators Association
https://nbmoa.org

National Business League, Inc
1001 Woodward Suite 910
Detroit, MI 48226
(313) 818-3017
https://nationalbusinessleague.org

National Coalition of Black Meeting Professionals
1800 Diagonal Road
Alexandria, VA 22314
(571) 366-1779
https://ncbmp.com

National Minority Supplier Development Council
1359 Broadway 10th Floor, Suite 1000
New York, NY 10018
(212) 944-2430
https://nmsdc.org

National Minority Business Council

National Urban League
80 Pine Street, 9th Floor
New York, NY 10005
(212) 558-5300
https://nul.org

Operation Hope Small-Business Empowerment Program
https://operationhope.org

Opportunity Fund
https://www.opportunityfund.org

Reign Venture Capital
https://www.reignvc.com

Rethink Education
https://rethink.vc/education

Rising Tide Capital
384 Martin Luther King Drive
Jersey City, NJ 07305
(201) 432-4316
https://www.risingtidecapital.org

Small Business Innovation Research (SBIR) and Small Business Technology Transfer (STTR) programs
https://sbir.nih.gov

Start Small. Think Big.
https://www.startsmallthinkbig.org

US Black Chambers

USDA Rural Business Development Grants
https://www.rd.usda.gov/programs-services/rural-business-development-grants

"Verify Black" Economic Justice Initiative
http://verifyblack.org

Funding & Resources for Black Women Entrepreneurs

Amber Grant
https://ambergrantsforwomen.com/get-an-amber-grant/

Cartier Women's Initiative
https://application-form.cartierwomensinitiative.com

Girlboss Foundation
https://www.girlboss.com/read/small-business-grants-for-women

Halstead Grant
https://grant.halsteadbead.com

Imanee
https://www.imanee.org

National Association of Colored Women's Clubs
https://www.nacwc.com

New Voices Fund
https://newvoicesfund.com

The Links Incorporate
1200 Massachusetts Avenue NW
Washington, DC 20005
(202) 842-8686
https://linksinc.org

Tory Burch Foundation Fellows Program
http://www.toryburchfoundation.org/fellows

Walker's Legacy Foundation
1865 Connecticut Avenue NW, Fl 10
Washington, DC 20009
https://www.walkerslegacy.org

Women Founders Network Fast Pitch Competition
https://www.womenfoundersnetwork.com

WORC
2010 Chestnut Street
Philadelphia, PA 19103
215-564-5500
http://www.worc-pa.com

Online Black Owned Directories and Resources

Bauce Magazine
https://baucemag.com

Black Business
https://www.blackbusiness.com

Black Connect Business
https://blackconnect.com

Black Enterprise
https://www.blackenterprise.com

Black Nation App
https://www.blacknation.app

Black News
https://www.blacknews.com

Black Pages
http://blackpages.com

Black Owned Brooklyn
https://www.blackownedbrooklyn.com

Black Owned Chicago
https://blackownedchicago.com

Black Owned New Jersey
blackownednj.com

Blavity
https://blavity.com

EatOkra (Black Owned Restaurant Finder & App)
https://www.eatokra.com

Essence
https://www.essence.com

I Am Black Business
https://iamblackbusiness.com

kweliTV
https://www.kweli.tv

Mars Reel
https://www.marsreel.com

Official Black Wall Street (Website & App)
https://officialblackwallstreet.com

Support Black Owned- SBO (Website & App)
https://www.supportblackowned.com

Ujuu Media
https://www.ujuumedia.com

Urban One
https://urban1.com

Watch The Yard
https://www.watchtheyard.com

Black Owned E-commerce

African Art World
http://www.africanartworld.com

Alaffia
https://www.alaffia.com

Art Jaz Gallery
http://www.artjaz.com

Avisca Art
http://www.avisca.com

Building Economic Advancement Network (BEAN)
https://www.iambean.us

Black Art In America
https://www.blackartinamerica.com

Black Art Auction
https://www.blackartauction.com

Black Art Depot
http://www.blackartdepot.com

Black-Owned Market
https://ourbom.com

BRK+GRN
https://blkgrn.com

Buy From A Black Woman
https://www.buyfromablackwoman.org

EcoVibe
https://ecovibestyle.com

Etsy (Black Owned)
https://www.etsy.com/search?q=black%20owned%20shops&ref=auto-1

Heritage Art
https://heritagesart.com

Momaa Art
https://momaa.org

Peace & Riot
http://www.peaceandriot.com

Saatchi Art
https://www.saatchiart.com/paintings/african-american-art

Shoppe Black
https://shoppeblack.us

The Nile List
https://www.thenilelist.com

Thrilling
https://shopthrilling.com

We Buy Black
https://webuyblack.com

Yellow Mountain Garden
https://www.yellowmountaingarden.com

Black Owned Supermarkets & Food Products

ONLINE SUPERMARKET & FOOD SERVICES
Agric Organics Urban Farming
https://www.agricorganics.com

Black and Mobile

https://www.blackandmobile.com

Callaloo Box
https://callaloobox.com

Forty Acres Fresh Market
https://www.fortyacresfreshmarket.com

Fresh Moves (Mobile Market)
Chicago, IL
info@freshmoves.org
http://www.freshmoves.org
Global Village Cuisine
https://globalvillagecuisine.com

Golden Krust
https://www.goldenkrust.com

Iya Foods
https://www.iyafoods.com

Ocean's 97
https://oceans97.com

Roots & Vine Produce and Cafe
https://rootsandvineinc.com

Trans Taylor
https://transtaylor.com

Yummy Spoonfuls (Organic Kids Food)
https://yummyspoonfuls.com

SUPERMARKETS
Circle Food Store
1522 St Bernard Avenue #1499
New Orleans, LA 70116
(504) 940-2111

Giant Eagle in East Hills
9001 Frankstown Road
Pittsburgh, PA 15235
(412) 371-0858

Grocery Outlet
2175 West, Rosecrans Avenue
Compton, CA 90222
(310) 667-5527

ONLINE PRODUCTS
(Alcoholic Beverages)

3 Parks Wine
https://3parkswine.com

18th Street Brewery
http://www.18thstreetbrewery.com

Berkshire Farms Winery
https://berkshirefarmswinery.com
Brazo Fuerte Brewing
http://brazo-fuerte.squarespace.com

Black Frog Brewery
https://blackfrogbrewery.com

Brown Estate Winery
https://www.brownestate.com

Cajun Fire Brewing Company
http://drinkcajunfire.com

Crowns and Hops Brewing Company
https://crownsandhops.com

DaleView Biscuits & Beer
https://www.biscuitsandbeer.nyc

Down Home Brewing Company
http://downhomebrewingcompany.com

Four City Brewing Co.
https://www.fourcitybrewing.com

Green Bench Brewing Company
https://www.greenbenchbrewing.com

Hackensack Brewing
https://www.hackensackbrewing.com

Harlem Blue Beer
https://www.harlemblue.com

Harlem Brewing Co.
https://www.harlembrewing.com

Harlem Hops Beer
https://harlemhops.com

Harris Family Brewery
https://www.harrisfamilybrewery.net

Jenny Dawn Cellars
https://www.jennydawncellars.com

Love Cork Screw Wines
https://lovecorkscrew.com

Khonso Brewing Company
http://khonsobrewing.com

Maison Noir Wines
https://maisonnoirwines.com

Métier Brewing Company
https://metierbrewing.com

McBride Sisters (Wine)
https://www.mcbridesisters.com

Montclair Brewery
https://www.montclairbrewery.com

New England Sweetwater Farm and Distillery
https://newenglandsweetwater.com

Patuxent Brewing Company
https://www.patuxentbrewing.com

Pur Noire Wines
https://purnoirewines.com

Rhythm Brewing Company
https://rhythmbrewingco.com

Sankofa Beer Company
https://www.sankofabeer.com

Soul Mega Beer
https://soulmega.com

Stuyvesant Champagne
https://www.stuyvesantchampagne.com

Theopolis Vineyards
https://www.theopolisvineyards.com

Uncle Nearest Whiskey
https://unclenearest.com

Union Craft Brewing
https://www.unioncraftbrewing.com

Warcloud Brewing
http://warcloudbrewing.com

Weathered Souls Brewing Company
http://weatheredsouls.beer

White Lion Brewing Company
https://whitelionbrewing.com

ZAFA Wines
https://zafawines.com

NON- ALCOHOLIC BEVERAGES
2T Waters
http://2twater.com

Adjourn Teahouse
https://www.adjournteahouse.com

Berry Bissap
https://www.berrybissap.com

BLK & Bold (Coffee)
https://blkandbold.com

Boss Blend Coffee
https://www.bossblendcoffee.com

Brooklyn Tea
https://brooklyntea.com

Cuples Tea House
https://cuplesteahouse.com

Chicago French Press (Coffee)
https://chicagofrenchpress.com

Dusable City Ancestral Winery & Vineyards and Dusable City Botanical Farms https://www.dusablecityancestralwinery.com

Ellis Island Tea
https://www.samsclub.com/p/jamaican-sweet-tea-6-pack-64-oz/prod21400266

Ivy's Tea Co.
https://www.ivystea.com

Positivity Alkaline Water
https://positivitywater.com

Red Bay Coffee
https://www.redbaycoffee.com

Scotty D's Coffee
https://www.scottydcoffee.com

SipSlow Tea (Loose Leaf Tea)
https://www.sipslowtea.com

Supreme Spring Water
https://www.supremespringwater.com

Tea Brew Farm
https://www.teabrewfarm.com

SWEETS & DESSERTS

B Cake NY
https://www.bcakeny.com

Baked Cravings
https://www.bakedcravings.com

Blondery
https://blondery.com

Delights by Dawn (Alcohol Infused Desserts)
https://delightsbydawn.com

Freak of Nature (Chocolate & Pudding)
https://www.freaksofnature.co.uk

Kay's Kookies
https://kayskookies.com

Maya's Cookies (Vegan Cookies)
https://www.mayascookies.com

Partake Cookies
https://partakefoods.com

Sol Cacao (Chocolate)
https://www.solcacao.com

Strafford Creamery
https://straffordcreamery.com

Swag Brownie Barz
https://www.swagbrowniebarz.com

Sweet Dames (Desserts)
https://sweetdames.com

The Furlough Cheesecake
https://thefurloughcheesecake.com

Tranquilitea Tea House
https://tranquiliteahouse.com

Tubby's Taste (Vegan Cookies)
https://www.tubbystaste.com

SNACK ITEMS

Aya Raw Snacks (Plant-Based)
https://www.ayaraw.com

Holmes Applesauce
https://homesapplesauce.com

LoAdebar (Energy Bar)
https://www.loadebar.com

Marjorie's Beef Jerky
http://www.marjoriesbeefjerky.com

Oh-Mazing Food (Granola Snacks)
https://www.ohmazingfood.com

Pipcorn (Popcorn)
https://www.pipsnacks.com

Project Pop (Organic Kettle Popcorn)
https://www.eatprojectpop.com

Sanaia Applesauce
https://tastesanaia.com

Symphony Chips
https://symphonychips.com

Tea Squares (Snack Bars)
https://www.teasquares.com

PANTRY ITEMS

A Dozen Cousins (Beans)
https://adozencousins.com

AubSauce (BBQ Sauce)
https://www.aubsauce.com

Berhan Teff Flour
https://berhan.co

Capital City Co. (Wing Sauce)
https://www.shopcapitalcity.com

Charleston Gourmet Burger Company (Burger Sauces & Marinade)
https://charlestongourmetburger.com

Essie Spice
https://www.essiespice.com

EXAU Olive Oil
https://exauoliveoil.com

Fineapple Vegan (Sauces & Spices)
https://fineapplevegan.com

Glory Foods (Sides & Spices)
https://www.gloryfoods.com

Habeeb's Gourmet Cooking Sauces
https://www.habeebssauce.com

Healthy on You (Spices)
https://www.healthyonyou.com

Jones Bar-B-Q (BBQ Sauce)
https://www.jonesbbqkc.com

Kyvan Foods (Salsa, Sauces, Spices, Jams, etc)
https://kyvan82.com

Lillie's of Charleston (BBQ Sauce)
https://www.lilliesofcharleston.com

Mama's Biscuits
https://mamabiscuit.com

Michele's Syrup (Breakfast and Dessert Syrup)
https://michelefoods.com

MylkDog (Nacho Sauce)
https://mylkdog.com

Neilly's Foods (Rice Mix)
https://neillys.com

Pitmaster LT's BBQ Sauce
https://pitmasterlt.com

Roots Holistic (Herbs & Spices)
https://www.rootsrva.com

Southern Culture Foods (Pancake & Waffle Mix/ Seasoning)
https://socukitchen.com

The Spice Suite
https://www.thespicesuite.com

Trade Street Jam Co. (Vegan Jam)
https://tradestjamco.com

Uncommon Bees (Honey)
https://www.uncommonbees.com

Vicky Cakes (Pancake & Waffle Mix)
https://www.vickycakesonline.com

Yolélé Foods (Cereal Grain)
https://www.yolele.com

Zach & Zoe Sweet Bee Farm Honey
https://zachandzoe.co

Black Owned Health Products & Resources

DISCLAIMER: Before using health products and services always consult with your doctor.

AARMY (Fitness)
https://www.aarmy.com

Alicia Archer (Yoga)
https://linktr.ee/kinkysweat

Banana Skirt (Fitness)
https://bananaskirt.net

Black Girl in OM (Mental Health)
https://www.blackgirlinom.com

Black Girls Breathing (Mental Health)
https://www.blackgirlsbreathing.com

Cactus Center (Mental Health)
https://cactuscenternj.com

Drop Squad Kitchen (Nutrition)
http://dropsquadkitchen.com

Fit with the Flow (Fitness)
https://fitwiththeflow1.vhx.tv

Grit by Brit (Fitness)
https://www.dallasgritfitness.com

Harlem Cycle (Fitness)
https://harlem-cycle.com

Healhaus (Mental Health)
https://www.healhaus.com

Heavenly Delight (Nutrition)
https://heavenlydelightcatering.com

Ingrid Clay (Fitness)
https://www.ingridsclay.com

Inner Workout (Mental Health)
https://www.innerworkout.co

Intentional Therapy (Mental Health)
https://www.intentionaltherapy.org

ISLY (Mental Health)
http://isly.org/meet-the-founder

James Brewer Body (Fitness)
https://www.brewerbody.com

Jeanette Jenkins (Fitness)
https://linktr.ee/msjeanettejenkins

Mama Glow (Maternal Health)
https://mamaglow.com

Motiva (Vitamins for Women)
https://www.movitaorganics.com

Muniq (Gut Health)
https://www.muniqlife.com

Naturade (Nutrition)
https://www.naturade.com

Nicole Lunan (Mental Health)
https://www.nicolevirtual.com

Oasis Wellness Group (Mental Health)
https://www.oasiswellnessgrp.org

Orange Moon (Nutrition)
https://www.the-orangemoon.com

Peak & Valley (Adaptogen Blends)
https://peakandvalley.co

Perspective (Mental Health)
https://tryperspective.com

Queen Shito
https://www.gloriasshito.com

Sacred Vibes Apothecary (Cleansing Products)
http://www.sacredvibeshealing.com

Salma Nakhlawi (Fitness)
https://linktr.ee/stronghergirls

Speir Pilates (Fitness)
https://www.speirpilates.com

Stretch22 (Fitness)
https://stretch22.com

Tatiana Grant LPC, NCC (Mental Health)
https://meredithobrienlcsw.com

The Beta Way (Mental Health)
https://www.thebetaway.net

The Black Doula (Maternal Health)
https://theblackdoula.com

The Healing Experience (Mental Health)
https://healingexperiencecounseling.org

The It Girl Message Therapy
https://www.theitgirlmassagetherapy.com

Thrive Health Lab (Fitness)
https://www.thrivehealthlab.com

Urban Asanas (Yoga)
https://www.urbanasanas.com

Vegan Smart (Plant Based Vegan Supplements)
https://www.vegansmart.com

Vibrant Health (E-Commerce Shop)
https://vibranthealth.com

Black Owned Farms

Abanitu Farm (Roxboro, NC)
http://www.abanituorganics.com

Annabessacook Farm (Winthrop, Maine)
http://annabessacookfarm.com

AM Lewis Farms (Matteson, IL)
https://www.amlewisfarms.com

Bain Home Garden (Rehoboth, AL)
https://bainhomegardens.com

Ballew Estates (Madison Co, Kentucky)
https://www.ballew-estates.org

Barbour Farm (Canmer, KY)
http://www.barboursfarm.harvesthand.com

Berrily Urban (Northern VA)
https://www.berrilyurban.com

Bladensburg Farm (Riverdale, MD)
http://www.ecoffshoots.org/programs/bladensburg-farm

Botanical Bites Provisions (Fredericksburg, VA)
https://www.botanicalbitesandprovisionsllc.com

Bonton Farms (Dallas, TX)
https://bontonfarms.org

Boyd Farms (Nathalie, VA)
http://www.johnboydjr.com

Broadrock Community Garden (Richmond, VA)
https://beautifulrva.org/broadrock-community-garden/

Brooklyn Rescue Mission Urban Harvest (Brooklyn, NY)
http://brmuhc.org

Caney Creek Ranch- Meat (Oakwood, TX)
https://farmtofreezermeat.com

Carter Family Farm (Unionville, VA)
http://thecarterfarms.com

Cherry Hill Urban Garden (Cherry Hill, MD)
https://cherryhillurbangarden.wordpress.com

City Slicker Farms (Oakland, CA)
https://www.cityslickerfarms.org

Chi City Foods (Chicago, IL)
https://www.chicityfoods.com

Clean Greens (Seattle, WA)
http://cleangreensfarm.com

Clemmons Family Farm (Charlotteville, VT)
http://www.clemmonsfamilyfarm.org

Corky's Nuts (Northern CA)
https://corkysnuts.com

Cryer's Family Produce (Mount Hermon, LA)
cryersfamilyproduce@gmail.com
(985) 335-5738

Cusheeba Earth: A Soil Culture Farm (Onley, VA)
https://cusheebaearth.tumblr.com

D-TownFarm (Detroit, MI)
https://www.d-townfarm.com

Daddy's Neighborhood Fresh Market
https://dnfmarket.weebly.com

Datus Henry Industries (Birmingham, AL)
https://datushenry.com

Darden Bridgeforth & Sons (Tanner, AL)
http://www.bridgeforthinternational.com

Deep Roots Farm (Brandywine, MD)
https://deeprootsfarm.us

Dodo Farms (Brookeville, MD)
https://www.dodofarmsmd.com

East New York Farms (Brooklyn, NY)
https://ucceny.org/enyf

First Fruits Farm (Louisburg, NC)
https://wisdomforlife.org/firstfruitsfarm

Fisher Farms (Jonesville, FL)
https://fisherfarms1939.square.site

Fitrah Farms (Central VA)
https://fitrahfarms.com

Flower Factory (Baltimore, MD)
walker.marsh@thaflowerfactory.com
(443) 502-0840

Foot Print Farms (Jackson, MS)
https://footprintfarmsms.com

Four Mother's Farm (Princess Anne, MD)
http://www.fourmothersfarm.com

Fourtee Acres (Enfield, NC)
https://fourteeacres.wixsite.com

Francis Flowers & Herbs Farm (Pickens, MS)
https://www.ilovepurecine.com

Free Haven Farms (Lawnside, NJ)
https://freeheaveneducationalfarms.com

Fresh Future Farm (North Charleston, SC)
https://www.freshfuturefarm.org

Fresh Life Organics (Houston, TX)
https://www.freshlifehtx.com

Go Greens Farms (Suffolk, VA)
https://www.gogreenfarms757.com

Good Sense Farm (Washington, DC)
info@goodsensefarm.com

Grafted Growers (Raleigh, NC)
https://graftedgrowers.com

Green Heffa Farms (Liberty, NC)
https://www.greenheffafarms.com

Griffin Organic Poultry (Harthorne, FL)
https://www.griffinorganicpoultry.com

Grow Baton Rouge (Baton Rouge, LA)
http://growbatonrouge.com

Gullah Farmers Cooperative (St. Helena Island, SC)
http://www.gullahfarmerscoop.org

Hattie Carthan Community Garden (Brooklyn, NY)
https://www.hattiecarthancommunitymarket.com

Hawk Mountain Earth Center (Newark, NJ)
https://www.hawkmountainearthcenter.org

Hawkins Homestead Farm (Kinsey, AL)
https://hawkinshomesteadfarm.com

Haynie Farms (Reedville, VA)
http://www.hayniefarms.com

Hyah Heights (Newark, NJ)
http://www.hyahheights.net/urban-garden-directory.html

Infinite Zion Roots Farms (Apopka, FL)
https://www.infinitezionfarms.org

Ital Life Farm (Tampa, FL)
https://itallifefarm.com

Jenny's Market (Friendship, MD)
https://www.jennysmarket.net

John H. Moody Farm (Soso, MS)
https://www.johnhmoodyfarm.com

Laketilly Acres (New Orleans, LA)
https://romeenterprise.wixsite.com/laketillyacres

Lettuce Live Urban Farm (Missouri City, TX)
https://www.lettucelive.org

Local Lands (Dublin, GA)
https://www.locallands.net

Long Walk Spring Farm (New Boston, TX)
https://www.longwalkspring.com

Mama Isis Farm & Market (Baton Rouge, LA)
https://mamaisisfarmandmarket.ecwid.com

Marlow Farms (Kissimmee, FL)
https://marlow-farms.com

Metro Atlanta Urban Farm (Royston, GA)
http://themetroatlantaurbanfarm.com

Mighty Thundercloud Edible Forest (Birdsnest, VA)
http://thundercloud.farm

Millbrook Urban Farms (Phoenix, AZ)
info@millbrookurbanfarms.com
(602) 821-8291

Mill Creek Farm (Philadelphia, PA)
https://www.millcreekurbanfarm.org

Miller City Farm (Fairburn, GA)
http://millercityfarm.com

Morning Glory Homestead Farm (St. Helena Island, SC)
https://www.morninggloryhomestead.com

Morris Gbolo's World Crop Farms (Vineland, NJ)
http://site.worldcropsfarm.com

Mother's Finest Urban Farms (Winston Salem, NC)
https://www.mothersfinesturbanfarms.com

Mudbone Grown (Portland, OR)
https://www.mudbonegrown.com

Nature's Candy Farm (Atlanta, GA)
https://naturescandyfarms.square.siteq2

Oko Vue Produce Co (New Orleans, LA)
https://www.makinggroceriesmarket.com

Patagonia Flower Farms (Patagonia, AZ)
https://www.patagoniaflowerfarm.com

Patchwork City Farms (Atlanta, GA)
https://www.patchworkcityfarms.com

Phat Beets Produce (Oakland, CA)
https://phatbeetsproduce.org

Philadelphia Urban Creators (Philadelphia, PA)
http://www.phillyurbancreators.org

Pine Knot Farms (Hillsborough, NC)
https://www.pineknotfarmsnc.com

Provost Farm (Iberia Parish, LA)
https://www.provostfarmllc.com

Rainshadow Organics (Sisters, OR)
https://www.rainshadoworganics.com

Rancho de Rodney (Fresno, CA)
(559) 412-2219

Rare Variety Farms (Columbia, SC)
https://www.rarevarietyfarms.com

RD & S Farm (Brandon, MS)
https://rdsfarm.wixsite.com/tradag

Rise & Root Farm (Chester, NY)
https://www.riseandrootfarm.com

Root Life (New Haven, CT)
https://www.rootlife.org

Project Rootz Farm (Phoenix, AZ)
https://www.projectrootsaz.org

Russellville Urban Gardening Project
(Russellville KY)
efuanjd@yahoo.com
(270) 847-8726

Savage Farms (Durham, NC)
http://www.bflt.org/savage-farm.html

SCF Organic Farms (Sumter, SC)
https://scforganicfarms.com

Scott Family Farms (Fresno, CA)
http://www.scottfamilyfarms.net

Semente Farm (Lithonia, GA)
https://www.sementefarm.com

Shire Gate Farm (Owensville, MO)
http://www.shiregatefarm.com

Sky Island Farm (Humptulips, WA)
https://skyislandfarmcsa.com

Slak Market Farm (Lexington, KY)
https://www.slakmarket.com

Smarter By Nature LLC (Tallahassee, FL)
https://www.smarterbynature.org

Soilful City (Washington, DC)
https://soilfulcitydc.wpcomstaging.com/2016/04/28/soilful-city-x-afro-ecology

Sola Food Co-op
http://www.solafoodcoop.com

Soul Fire Farm (Petersburg, NY)
https://www.soulfirefarm.org

Swanson Family Farm (Hampton, GA)
https://www.swansonfamilyfarmllc.com

Sylvanaqua Farms (Washington, DC/Norfolk, VA)
https://www.sylvanaqua.com

Three Part Harmony (Washington, DC)
http://threepartharmonyfarm.org

Tiger Mountain Foundation (Phoenix, AZ)
http://www.tigermountainfoundation.org

Truly Living Well (Atlanta, GA)
https://www.trulylivingwell.com

Vanguard Ranch (Gordonsville, VA)
https://vanguard-ranch-natural-gourmet.ueniweb.com

Ward's Farm (Salem, NJ)
http://wardsfarmnj.com

We Over Me Farm (Dallas, TX)
https://www.pqc.edu/farm

Black Owned Personal Products

OVERALL COSMETICS
AJ Crimson Beauty
https://ajcimson.com

Beauty Bakerie
https://www.beautybakerie.com

BLAC Minerals
https://www.blacminerals.com

Black Opal
https://blackopalbeauty.com

Bossy Cosmetics
https://bossybeauty.com

Camara AUnique Beauty (Eye Lashes)
https://www.camaraaunique.com

Colour U Cosmetics
https://www.facebook.com/colourucosmetics

Coloured Raine
https://colouredraine.com

Danessa Myricks Beauty
https://www.danessamyricksbeauty.com

Dope Coffee
https://www.realdope.coffee

epi.logic
https://www.brooklynfaceandeye.com

Fenty Beauty
https://www.fentybeauty.com

GlōGirl Cosmetics
https://www.glogirlcosmetics.com

Hue Noir
https://huenoir.com

IMAN Cosmetics
https://imancosmetics.com

Joséphine Cosmetics
https://josephinecosmetics.com

Juvia's Place
https://www.juviasplace.com

Lamik Beauty
https://loveyubi.com

Lauren Napier Beauty (Face Wipes)
https://www.laurennapier.com

Makeda K Beauty
https://makedakbeauty.com

Makeup by Sparkle
https://www.makeupbysparkle.com

Mented Cosmetics
https://www.mentedcosmetics.com

OMGLO Cosmetics
https://omglocosmetics.com

Pat McGrath Labs
https://www.patmcgrath.com

The Crayon Case
https://www.thecrayoncase.com

Quon's Eyes (Eye Lashes)
https://www.quonseyes.com

UOMA Beauty
https://uomabeauty.com

Yubi (Make-up Brush)
https://loveyubi.com

LIPS

127East
https://www.127east.com

Celfie Cosmetics
https://celfiecosmetics.com

Essentials by Edwina Kulego
https://essentialsbyedwina.com

Gold Label Cosmetics
https://www.goldlabelcosmetics.com

LIPP Beauty (Artistry)
https://www.fetebylippbeauty.com

Makeup For Melanin Girls (MFMG)

https://makeupformelaningirls.com

Stay Golden Cosmetics
https://staygoldencosmetics.com

The Lip Bar
https://thelipbar.com

NAILS

25th & June
https://www.25thandjune.com

Adore'her Nails
https://www.adorehernails.com

Auda B
https://audabbeauty.com

Bernadette Thompson
https://www.bernadettethompson.com

Breukelen Polished
https://www.bkpolished.com

D.I.D Nail Paint
https://www.getyournailsdid.com

Ginger & Liz
https://www.gingerandliz.com

Janet & Jo
https://www.janetandjo.com

La Pierre Cosmetics
https://lapierrecosmetics.com

Law Beauty Essentials
https://www.lawbeautyessentials.com

Lisa Nail Lacquer
https://www.lisalacquer.com

Mischo Beauty
https://www.mischobeauty.com

Pear Nova
https://www.pearnova.com

People of Color
https://www.peopleofcolorbeauty.com

Polish and Co
https://polishandco.com

Suite Eleven
https://www.suiteleven.com

Triple O Polish
https://www.ooopolish.com

HAIR ACCESSORIES, TEXTURES, & LOCS

Afra Hair Jewelry
https://www.afranyc.com

Baby Tress (Edge Styler)
https://babytress.com

Boho Locs (Locs)
https://boholocs.com

Brush With the Best (Brushes, Combs)
https://www.brushwiththebest.com

Canviiy (Scalp Care)
https://canviiy.com

Cee Cee's Closet (Wraps, Coverings, etc)
https://www.ceeceesclosetnyc.com

Chocolate Kinks & Kurls
https://chocolatekinksandkurls.com

Curls
https://curls.biz

Curls Dynasty
https://curlsdynasty.com

Curlbox
https://curlbox.com

Curl Mix
https://www.curlmix.com

Dr. Locs (Locs)
https://drlocs.com

Glow by Daye (Wraps, Bonnets, Caps, Scarves)
https://www.glowbydaye.com

Grace Eleyae (Wraps, Pillows)
https://www.graceeleyae.com

Hairbrella (Rain Hat Reinvented)
https://hairbrella.com

Kinky-Curly
https://kinky-curly.com

Kinky Tresses
https://kinkytresses.com

Luxju
https://www.luxjunaturalhairproducts.com

Miss Jessie's
https://missjessies.com

Ooli Beauty (Locs)
https://oolibeauty.com

Runaway Curls
https://www.runwaycurls.com

The Cut Buddy
https://thecutbuddy.com

The Hair Pillow
https://www.lifestylepillows.com

Wrap Life (Wraps)
https://thewrap.life

HAIR

Adwoa Beauty
https://www.adwoabeauty.com

Alikay Naturals
https://alikaynaturals.com

Alodia Hair Care
https://alodiahaircare.com

Bask & Bloom Essentials
https://baskandbloomessentials.com

Beauty by Dr.Kari
https://www.beautybydrkari.com

Black Girl Long Hair (BGLH)
https://bglh-marketplace.com

Bouclème
https://www.boucleme.co.uk

Briogeo
https://briogeohair.com

Bye Bye Parabens
https://www.byebyeparabens.com

Design Essentials
https://designessentials.com

Ecoslay
https://www.ecoslay.com

Eden Body Works
https://edenbodyworks.com

E'TAE Natural Products
https://www.etaeproducts.com

Girl and Hair
https://www.girlandhair.com

Hair Rules
https://hairrules.com

Her Given Hair
https://www.hergivenhair.com

Jane Carter Solution
https://janecartersolution.com

Kaleidoscope Hair Products
https://iluvcolors.com

Luster's Pink
https://www.lusterspink.com

Manketti Oil Haircare Range
https://charlottemensah.com

Mayvenn

https://shop.mayvenn.com

Melanin Haircare
https://melaninhaircare.com

Meraki Organics
https://shopmerakiorganics.com

MICHE Beauty
https://www.michebeauty.com

Mielle Organics
https://mielleorganics.com

Mo Knows Hair
https://moknowshair.com

Myavana
https://www.myavana.com

Nancy's Kitchen Products
https://www.nancyskitchenproducts.co

Naturally Me and You
https://naturallyyounme.com

Naturalicious
https://naturalicious.net

Organi Grow Hair Co.
https://organigrowhairco.com

Pattern Beauty
https://patternbeauty.com

Qhemet Biologics
https://www.qhemetbiologics.com

Rucker Roots
https://ruckerroots.com

Shea Moisture
https://www.sheamoisture.com

Shear Genius Collection
https://deeperthanhair.com

Sienna Naturals
https://www.siennanaturals.com

Soultanicals
https://soultanicals.com

Strands of Faith
https://strandsoffaith.com

Tailored Beauty
https://www.tailoredbeautyproducts.com

Taliah Waajid Natural Hair
https://naturalhair.org

Thank God It's Natural (tgin)
https://thankgoditsnatural.com

The Doux
https://thedoux.com

The Mane Choice
https://themanechoice.com

TPH by Taraji
https://tphbytaraji.com

TreLuxe
https://discovertreluxe.com

Twisted Sista
https://www.twistedsista.com

Uhai
https://uhaihair.com

Uncle Funky's Daughter
https://unclefunkysdaughter.com

Vernon Francois
https://www.vernonfrancois.com

UNISEX PERSONAL CARE
Black Soap Club
https://blacksoap.club

Buttah Skincare
https://www.buttahskin.com

Camille Rose
https://www.camillerose.com

Coral Oral Toothbrushes
https://coraloral.com

Dirt Don't Hurt
https://dirtdonthurtme.com

Foot Nanny
https://footnanny.com

Garner's Garden
https://garnersgarden.com

H.Lee Body Essentials
https://www.hleebodyessentials.com

Honey Dipped Essentials
https://www.honey-dipped.com

Ivyees
https://www.ivyees.com

Karite
https://www.mykarite.com

KLUR
https://klur.co

Koils By Nature
https://www.koilsbynature.com

Lalin et La Sirèn
https://lalinetlasiren.com

Ounce of Nature
https://ounceofnature.com

Oyin Handmade
https://oyinhandmade.com

Pardo Naturals
https://pardonaturals.com

Plant Apothecary
https://plantapothecary.com

Products by Lizzie
https://www.productsbylizzie.com/collections/all

Shimirose
https://shimirose.com

Soap Distillery
https://soapdistillery.com

Southern Handmade Essentials
https://shessentials17.com

The Ph Company
https://www.quintessentialsgroup.com/collections/oral-bundles

Tropic Isle Living
https://tropicisleliving.com

Urban Hydration
https://www.urbanhydration.com

PERSONAL CARE FOR WOMEN

Aba Love Apothecary
https://www.abaloveapothecary.com

Adiva Naturals
https://adivanaturals.com

AHF Body Chemistry
https://www.ahfbodychemistry.com

Alchemy Body Shop
https://www.alchemybodyshop.com

Anne's Apothecary
https://annesapothecary.com

Base Butter
https://www.basebutter.com

Beija Flor Naturals
https://www.beijaflornaturals.com

Brown Butter Beauty
https://www.brownbutterbeautyshop.com

Chloe and Chad
https://www.chloeandchad.com

Ebi (Maternal Care)
https://www.weareebi.com

Emanate Essentials
https://www.emanateessentials.com

Fran's Bodycare
https://fransbodycare.com

Foxie Cosmetics
https://foxiecosmetics.com

Gilded
https://gildedbody.com

Golde
https://golde.co

Hairizon
https://www.hairizonbeauty.com

Happy Girl Products
https://happygirl.shop/products

Home Body
https://www.homebodyworld.com

KNC Beauty
https://kncbeauty.com

Iyoba
https://www.iyoba.com

Jacq's
https://www.shopjacqs.com

Jade & Fox Co.
https://www.jadefox.co

Kaike
https://www.shopkaike.com

Karen's Body Beautiful
https://www.karensbodybeautiful.com

Lauryn's Garden
https://laurynsgarden.com

Limegreen
https://www.brooklynlimegreen.com

Maison 276
https://maison276.com

Mary Louise Cosmetics
https://www.mymarylouise.com

Matrescence
https://www.matrescenceskin.com

Mixed Chicks
https://mixedchicks.net

Motherland Essentials
https://www.motherlandessentials.com

OBIA Naturals
https://www.obianaturals.com

Olive Branch
https://www.shoptheolive.com

Play Pits
https://playpits.com

The Honey Pot
https://thehoneypot.co

Temple Zen
https://yourtemplezen.com

Touch of Body
https://evoketouch.com

PERSONAL CARE FOR MEN
Bevel
https://getbevel.com

Boyface
https://boyfaceme.com

Burke Avenue
burkeavenue.com

Ceylon Skincare
ceylonskincare.com

Dr. Goat
https://www.drgoatbfc.com

Frederick Benjamin
https://shop.frederickbenjamin.com

Hammer & Nails
https://hammerandnailsgrooming.com

Himistry
https://himistry.com

Mantl
https://www.mantlmen.com

Murray's
http://www.murrayspomade.com

Nature Boy
https://natureboyproducts.com

Scotch Porter
https://www.scotchporter.com

Solo Noir
https://solonoirformen.com

SKINCARE FOR WOMEN

Aba Love
https://www.abaloveapothecary.com

AbsoluteJoi
https://www.absolutejoi.com

Agrestal Beauty
https://agrestalbeauty.com

Ayele & Co.
https://ayele.co

BeautyStat Cosmetics
https://www.beautystat.com

Beneath Your Mask
https://beneathyourmask.com

Black Girl Sunscreen
https://www.blackgirlsunscreen.com

Blade + Bloom
https://bladeandbloom.com

Bolden
https://www.boldenusa.com

Brown Girl Jane
https://www.browngirljane.com

Butter by Keba
https://butterbykeba.com

Dehiya Beauty
https://dehiyabeauty.com

Elements of Aliel
https://www.elementsofaliel.com

Elle Johnson Co.
https://www.ellejohnson.co

Epara
https://www.eparaskincare.com

EveryHue Beauty
https://www.target.com/s?searchTerm=EveryHue+Beauty

GlowRx Skincare
https://www.glowrxskin.com

Good Beauté
https://goodbeaute.com

Grn Goods
https://grngoods.co

Hanahana Beauty
https://www.hanahanabeauty.com

Hyper Skin
https://gethyperskin.com

Kanti
https://kanti.us

Kayaire
https://www.kayaire.com

Kubra Kay Skincare
https://www.kubrakayskincare.com

Ladybug Skincare
https://ladybugskincare.com

Liha Beauty
https://lihabeauty.com

Marla Rene Skincare
https://marlarene.com

Noire Beauté
https://noirebeautebar.com

Nolaskinsentials
https://www.nolaskinsentials.com

nyakio Skincare
https://www.nyakio.com

Oui the People
https://www.ouithepeople.com

Paula's Whipp
https://www.paulaswhipp.com

Pholk Beauty
https://pholkbeauty.com

Range Beauty
https://www.rangebeauty.com

Redoux NYC
https://redoux.nyc

Rose Ingleton MD Skincare
https://www.rosemdskin.com

Rosen Skincare
https://www.rosenskincare.com

SkinBUTTR
https://skinbuttr.com

Topicals
https://mytopicals.com

True Moringa
https://truemoringa.com

Unsun
https://www.unsuncosmetics.com

Yelle Skincare
https://yelleskincare.com

FRAGRANCE

Amourdee Fragrances for Women
https://www.amourdeefragrances.com

Anu Essentials for Women
https://anuessentials.com

Chris Collins for Men
https://worldofchriscollins.com

Kimberly New York for Women
https://www.kimberlynewyork.com

Kirk Eliott Experience for Men
https://www.thekirkeliottexperience.com/collections/all

Le Bijoux Parfum for Women
https://www.lebijouxparfum.com

Maya Nije for Women
http://www.mayanjie.com

Motif Olfactif for Women
https://www.motifolfactif.com

Muse for Women
https://www.museexperiences.com/shop

Nick Ricardo Collection for Men
https://www.nickricardocollection.com/products/onyx

Ovation for Men
http://ovationfragrance.com

Savoir Faire for Men

https://savoirfaire.store

Zavies Women's Enamor Eau de Parfum Spray
https://zavies.com/collections/all

Black Owned Household Goods

TOILET PAPER & CLEANERS
Earthlymart Bathroom Cleaner
https://www.earthlymart.com

Freedom Paper Company LLC
https://fpcpower.com

Good Vibes Cleaning Products
https://www.goodvibesclean.com

LooHoo (Dryer Balls)
https://www.loo-hoo.com

Mommy Wipes:
https://mommywipe.com

Pur Home
https://pur-home.com

Reel Toilet Paper
https://reelpaper.com

The Green Laundress
http://thegreenlaundress.com/buy-now.html

The Hoot Cleaning Products
https://www.thehootallnatural.com

True Laundry Detergent
https://www.thetrueproducts.com

Ultra Kosmic Toilet Paper
https://www.ultrakosmic9.com

HOME TEXTILES
Bolé Road Textiles
https://boleroadtextiles.com

Lakay Designs
https://www.lakaydesigns.com

FURNISHINGS
AphroChic
https://www.aphrochic.com

AptDeco
https://www.aptdeco.com

Claude Home
https://www.claudehome.com

Global Attic
https://www.globalattic.com

Home By Be
https://www.homebybe.com

Jomo Furniture
https://www.jomofurniture.com

Karen Jai Home
https://karenjaihome.com

Lam Label
https://www.thelamlabel.com

Lichen
https://www.lichennyc.com

Sabai Design
https://sabai.design

ZEN Succulent
https://thezensucculent.com

KITCHEN
54Kibo (Dinnerware)
https://54kibo.com

Ekua Ceramics (Cups, Dishes, etc)
https://www.ekuaceramics.com

Estelle Colored Glass
https://www.estellecoloredglass.com

Karibe (Cookware)
https://karibecompany.com

Lolly Lolly Ceramics (Cups)
https://lolly-lolly.com/shop

Yowie (Cups, Dishes, etc)
https://www.shopyowie.com

HOME DECOR
Aya Paper Co
https://ayapaper.co

Black Pepper Paperie Co
https://shopbppco.com

Black Home
https://www.theblackhome.com

BLK MTK Vintage
https://www.blkmktvintage.com/collections/frontpage

Clare (Paint)
https://www.clare.com

Domain by Laura Hodges Studio
https://www.domainbylaurahodgesstudio.com

Don't Sleep Interiors (Decorate Pillows)
http://dontsleepinteriors.com

Duett Interiors (Decorative Pillows)
https://www.duettinteriors.com/shop

Effortless Composition
https://effortlesscomposition.com

Expedition Subsahara
https://www.expeditionsubsahara.com

FaceMadics
https://www.facemadics.com

Godly Gorgeous
http://www.godlygorgeous.com/shop-online

Goodee
https://www.goodeeworld.com

Hello Allison Art
https://helloallisonart.com

Jade Purple Brown
https://shop.jadepurplebrown.com

Johanna Howard Home
https://www.johannahoward.com

Jungalow
https://www.jungalow.com

Kashmir VIII
http://www.kashmirviii.com/products

Linoto
https://www.linoto.com

Malene Barnett
http://malenebarnett.com

Marie Burgos
https://www.marieburgosdesignthestore.com

Mitchell Black
https://mitchellblack.com

Pardon My Fro
https://pardonmyfro.com

Rayo & Honey
https://rayoandhoney.com/index.php/product-category/pennants

Reflektion Design
https://www.reflektiondesign.com

Robin Wilson Home
https://robinwilsonhome.com

Rochelle Porter
http://www.rochelleporter.com

Ron Nicole
https://www.ronnicole.com

SampleHAUS
https://www.mysamplehaus.com

Sheila Bridges
https://www.sheilabridges.com

SustainAble Home Goods
https://yoursustainablehome.com

Tal & Bert
https://talandbert.com

Tactile Matter
https://www.tactilematter.com

Under The Sunlight
https://underthesunlight.com

Wildfang Home
https://wildfanghome.com

xN Studio
http://www.osxnasozi.com

CANDLES

Alexandra Winbush
https://www.alexandrawinbush.com

Antik Lakay
https://www.antiklakay.com

Carmella Carter Candles
https://carmellacarter.com

Flickerwick Limited
https://flickerwicklimited.com

Harlem Candle Co.
https://www.harlemcandlecompany.com

Kintsugi Candle Co.
https://www.kintsugicandleco.com

KSM Candle Co.
https://www.knitssoyandmetal.com

Lit Brooklyn
https://www.litbklyn.co

Lomar Farms
https://www.lomarfarms.com

Love Notes Fragrances
https://lovenotesfragrances.com

Māktub Studio
https://maktubstudio.co

NaturalAnnie Essentials
https://www.naturalannieessentials.com

Posh Candle Co.
https://poshcandleco.com

Poze Candle Co.
https://pozecandle.com

Pretty Honest Candles
https://www.prettyhonestshop.com

Simple Scents Candle Company
https://www.simplyscentsbyshan.com

The 125 Collection
https://the125collection.com

Black Owned Cleaning & Design Services

Bailey Li Interiors (NYC)
https://www.designedbybaileyli.com

Eneia White Interiors (Orange, NJ)
https://www.eneiawhite.com

Esteam Carpet Clean (Atlanta, GA)
https://www.esteamcleannow.com

Cleaning Up With The Joneses (Lindenwold, NJ)
http://Jonesfamilycleaning.com

Goldfinch Cleaning Services (Bloomfield, N)
https://www.goldfinchcleaning.com

Maid Karma Home Cleaning (Laurel, MD)

https://maidkarma.com

Nicole Crowder Upholstery (DC)
https://www.nicolecrowderupholstery.com

Olọrọ Interiors (Philadelphia, PA)
https://www.olorointeriors.com

Powerhouse Medical Cleaning (Piscataway, NJ)
https://www.powerhousemedicalcleaning.com

Prestigious Cleaning (Gardena, CA)
https://www.prestigiouscleaningservices.com

Simply Subordinate (NJ)
https://www.simplysubordinate.com

Sole Organizer (DC)
https://www.soleorganizer.com

Taylor'd Maids Janitorial Services (Peachtree City, GA)
https://www.tmjsclean.com

Too Green Cleaning (New Brunswick, NJ)
https://toogreencleaning.com

Unhampered Laundry (Lamberville, NJ)
https://www.unhamperedlaundry.com

Whitney J Décor (New Orleans, LA)
https://whitneyjdecor.com

Black Owned Apparel Companies

JEWELRY
1929 Galore
https://1929galore.com

Auvere
https://auvere.com

Bernard James
https://bernardjames.com

JeBlanc
https://www.jeblanc.com/home

Johnny Nelson
http://johnnynelson.nyc

Lafalaise Dion Jewelry
https://lafalaise-dion.afrikrea.com/en

Melanie Marie Jewelry Collection
https://jewelry.melaniemarie.com

Octave Jewelry
https://octavejewelry.com

Third Crown
https://www.thirdcrown.com

Valerie Madison Fine Jewelry
https://www.valeriemadison.com

BAGS, LUGGAGE, & SHOES
Agnes Baddoo
https://www.agnesbaddoo.com

Aminah Abdul Jillil Shoes
https://aminahabduljillil.com

Anima Iris Bags
https://animairis.com/collections

Bruve Glen
https://bruceglen.com

F&W Style
https://www.fwstyle.com/collections/all

Fini Shoes
https://www.fini.shoes

Kahmune
https://kahmune.com

Kintu New York
https://www.kintunewyork.com

Laurus
https://www.laurus-online.com

Love, Cortnie

http://lovecortnie.com

Lovely Earthlings
http://www.lovelyearthlings.com

Made Leather Co.
https://madeleathercompany.com

Melah Boutique
https://www.melahboutique.com

Mifland
https://mifland.com

MWR Collection
https://www.mwrcollection.com/store

Petit Kouraj Bags
https://www.petitkouraj.com

Salone Monet Shoes
https://www.salonemonet.com

Shop The Collectionn
https://shopthecollectionn.com/collections/all

Shy Diva
https://shydiva.co

Sonique Saturday
https://www.soniquesaturday.com

Soul Seed
https://soulseedapparel.com/collections/black-pride-travel-bags

Stitched By Sukie
https://www.stitchedbysukie.com

The Purple Vault
https://www.thepurplevault.co/collections/all

Tippy Tot Shoes
https://tippytotshoes.com

Tote & Carry
https://www.totencarry.com

Vavvoune Bags
https://www.vavvoune.com

Yvonne Kone
https://www.yvonnekone.com

Zashadu Bags
https://www.zashadu.com/shop

UNISEX

A. Sauvage
https://asauvage.com/the-house

Ahluwalia Studio
https://www.ahluwaliastudio.com

Art Comes First
https://www.artcomesfirst.com

Ashya
http://www.ashya.co

Casely Hayford
https://casely-hayford.com

Chic Geeks (Apple Product Cases)
https://chicgeeks.com

Coco & Breezy Sunglasses
https://cocoandbreezy.com

Cross Colours
https://crosscolours.com

Daily Paper
https://www.dailypaperclothing.com

Diyanu
https://www.diyanu.com

Diop
https://weardiop.com

Dope on Arrival NYC
https://www.dopeonarrivalnyc.com

Fear of God
https://fearofgod.com

HGC Apparel
https://hgcapparel.com

House of Aama
https://houseofaama.com

Ih Nom Uh Nit
https://www.ihnomuhnit.co

Karl Kani
https://www.karlkani.com

Khiry
https://www.khiry.com/store

Kristopher Kites
https://kristopherkites.com

L'Enchanteur
https://www.lenchanteur.co

LIV Streetwear
https://livstreetwear.com/collections

Maxhosa Africa
https://maxhosa.africa

Melaninful
https://melaninful.net

Mon Cheri
https://www.officialmoncheri.com

Off-White
https://www.off---white.com/en-us

Oma the Label
https://www.omathelabel.com

Paskho
https://paskho.com

Patta
https://www.patta.nl

Places + Faces
https://www.placesplusfaces.com/collections

Pro Standard
https://teamprostandard.com

Pseudonym
https://www.bypseudonym.com/store

Pyer Moss
https://pyermoss.com

Rebels to Dons
https://www.rebelstodons.com/shop

Romeo Hunte
https://www.romeohunte.com

Sankofa Athletics
https://sankofaathletics.com/collections

Soundoff
https://www.soundoffdesign.com

Spergo
https://spergo.com

Studio 189
https://studiooneeightynine.com

Stuzo Clothing
https://www.stuzoclothing.com

Telfar
http://www.telfar.net

The Folklore
https://www.thefolklore.com

The Marathon Clothing
https://www.themarathonclothing.com

Tier NYC
https://www.shoptier.nyc

Tongoro
https://www.tongoro.com

Wales Bonner
https://walesbonner.net

Walker Wear
https://walkerwear.com

Waraire
https://waraire.com

XULY.bet
https://www.xulybet.com

Yam NYC
https://www.yamnyc.com

Yeezy
https://www.yeezysupply.com

WOMEN ATHLETIC, SWIM, LINGERIE AND SLEEP WEAR

Castamira (Swimsuits)
https://www.castamira.com

Cherry Blossom Intimates (Breast Prosthetics)
https://cherryblossomintimates.com

Culture Fit (Athletics)
https://www.culturefitclothing.com

Jade Swim (Swimwear)
https://jadeswim.com

Kemetic Knowledge (Athletics)
https://www.kemeticknowledge.com

Love, Vera (Lingerie)
https://www.lovevera.com

Nubian Skin (Lingerie)
https://us.nubianskin.com

Nude Barre (Lingerie)
https://nudebarre.com

Prayers and Plans (Sleepwear)
https://prayersandplans.co

Pru Apparel (Athletics)
https://www.pruapparel.com

Rec Room (Athletics)
https://rec-room.com/summer-of-comfort

Riot Swim (Swimwear)
https://www.riotswim.com

Tranz Fit Apparel (Athletics)
https://www.tranzfitapparel.com

Trap Yoga (Athletics)
www.itsyogabae.com

Zoezi (Athletics)
https://zoezisport.com

WOMEN

Amyang Fashun
https://www.amyang.com

Andrea Iyamah
https://www.andreaiyamah.com

Asata Maisé
https://www.asatamaise.com

Baby Phat
https://babyphat.com

Bephie's Beauty Supply
https://bephiesbeautysupply.com

Bfyne
https://bfyne.com

Brother Vellies
https://brothervellies.com

Carlton Yaito
https://carltonyaito.com

Cheyenne Kimora
https://www.cheyennekimora.com

Chinero Nnamani
https://www.chineronnamani.com

Christopher John Rogers

https://www.net-a-porter.com/en-us/shop/designer/christopher-john-rogers

Cushnie
https://www.cushnie.com

Diarra Blu
https://diarrablu.com

Edas
https://edas.store

Fenoel
https://fenoel.com

Fly By Knight
https://shopflybyknight.com

Grass-Fields
https://www.grass-fields.com

Hanifa
https://hanifa.co

Island Tribe
https://islandtribeusa.com

Jam & Rico
https://www.jamandrico.com

Kimberly Goldson
https://kimberlygoldson.com

LaQuan Smith
https://laquansmith.com

LaSette
https://www.lasette.shop

LavieByCk
https://laviebyck.com

LemLem
https://www.lemlem.com

Lukafit
https://lukafit.com

Mateo New York
https://mateonewyork.com

Matte Brand
https://shopmatte.com/collections

Mowalola
https://www.mowalola.com/shop2

Meuhleder
https://www.muehleder.com

Nichole Lynel
https://shopnicholelynel.com

Rebecca Allen
https://rebecca-allen.com

ReLove SF
https://shoprelove.com

Samaria Leah
https://samarialeah.com

Sammy B Designs
sammybdesigns.com

Sincerely Tommy
https://sincerelytommy.com

Stella Jean
https://www.stellajean.it

T.A New York
https://shop-ta.com

The K Label
https://theklabel.com

The Sixes (Tall Women)
https://www.thesixes.com

Thebe Magugu
https://www.thebemagugu.com

TLZ Femme
https://www.tlzlf.com

Tracy Reese
https://hopeforflowers.com

Victor Glemaud
https://www.glemaud.com

Voluptuous Clothing
https://voluptuousclothing.com

Undra Celeste New York
https://www.undracelesteny.com

William Okpo
https://williamokpo.com/collections

MEN

4Hunnid
https://4hunnid.com

10 Deep
https://10deep.com/collections

A Cold Wall
https://a-cold-wall.com

All Caps Studio
https://www.allcapstudio.com

Armando Cabral
https://shop.armando-cabral.com

Bel-Air Athletics
https://belairathletics.com

Bianca Saunders
https://www.biancasaunders.com

Billionaire Boys Club
https://www.bbcicecream.com

Brandon Blackwood New York
https://www.brandonblackwood.com

Brett Johnson
https://brettjohnson.co

Bricks and Wood
https://bricksandwood.us

Brownstone
https://brwnstne.co

Carrots by Anwar Carrots
https://anwarcarrots.com/collections

Come Back as a Flower
https://www.cbaaf.org

Darryl Brown
https://darrylbrown.com/collections

Diet Starts Monday
https://www.dietstartsmonday.us/collections

Dyne
https://dyne.life

Fat Tiger
https://www.fattigerworkshop.com

Frere
https://www.frereny.com

FTP
https://fuckthepopulation.com

FUBU
https://fubu.com

Gallery Dept.
https://gallerydept.com/collections

Golf Wang
https://golfwang.com

Heron Preston
https://www.heronpreston.com/en/US

Just Don
https://justdon.com

Kenneth Nicholson
https://www.kennethnicholson.us

Maki Oh
https://www.makioh.com

Martine Rose
https://martine-rose.com

Michel Men
https://www.michelmen.com

Nicholas Daley
https://nicholasdaley.net

No Name
https://www.noname-brand.com

Oliver Rogers
https://www.olivierofficial.com

Orange Culture
https://orangeculture.com.ng/shop

Phlemuns
http://www.phlemuns.com

Post Imperial
https://post-imperial.com

Renowned LA
https://www.renowned.la/webstore

Resurrect by Night
https://www.resurrectbynight.com

Roca Wear
https://www.rocawear.com

Saint Avenue
https://www.saintavenue.co

Sean John
https://seanjohn.com

Sheila Rashid
https://www.sheilarashid.com

Snooper Market
https://www.snoopermarket.com

Supervsn
https://supervsn.com/collections

The Brooklyn Circus
https://thebkcircus.com/collections

The Good Company
https://www.97allen.com

Union Los Angeles
https://store.unionlosangeles.com

WafflesNCream
https://wafflesncream.co.uk/collections/baffs

Who Decides War
https://whodecideswar.com/collections

X of Pentacles
https://xofpentacles.com

Black Owned Kid, Games & Toy Companies

Actually Curious Game
https://www.actuallycurious.com

Afrobets Flashcards
https://afrobets.square.site

Beautiful Curly Me
https://beautifulcurlyme.com

Because of Zoe
https://www.becauseofzoe.com

Brooklyn Lighthouse
https://breukelynthreads.com

Brown Toy Box
https://www.browntoybox.com

Cards for All People
https://cardsforallpeople.com

Coco'Pie Clothing
https://cocopieclothing.com

Confidence
https://gabbybows.com

Cooper Rose
https://cooperrosebaby.com

Crunchy Boutique
https://crunchyboutique.net

Darlyng & Co.
https://www.darlyngandco.com

Dionne Gooding
https://www.dionnegooding.com

Double Dutch Dolls
http://doubledutchdolls.com

Dreams and Jammies (Pajamas for Girls)
https://dreamsandjammies.com

Ehbuny Toys
https://ehbunytoys.com

Fun Weird Science
https://funweirdscience.com

Happy Mango
https://shophappymango.com

HarperIman Dolls
https://www.harperiman.com

HBCU Pride & Joy
https://hbcupridejoy.com

Healthy Roots Dolls
https://healthyrootsdolls.com

HerStory Doll
http://www.herstorydoll.com

Ikuzi Dolls
https://www.ikuzidolls.com

Just Like Me! Box
https://www.justlikemebox.com

KaAn's Designs
https://www.kaansdesigns.com

Kido Chicago
https://www.kidochicago.com

Kids Swag
https://kidsswag.ca

Kinara Park Kids
https://kinaraparkkids.com

King & Lola
https://kingandlola.com

Little Likes Kids
https://www.littlelikeskids.com

Little Muffincakes Baby Boutique
https://littlemuffincakes.com

Malaville Dolls
https://www.malavilletoys.com

Miles and Milan
https://milesandmilan.com

Natural Girls United
http://www.naturalgirlsunited.com

Neon Kisses
https://neonkissesinc.com

Pint Size Faith
https://www.pintsizefaith.com

Pooters Diapers
https://pootersdiapers.com

Pretty Brown Girl
https://prettybrowngirlshop.com

Pretty Please Teethers
https://www.prettypleaseteethers.com

Puzzle Huddle
https://puzzlehuddle.com

Ozzie + Olive
https://ozzieolive.bigcartel.com

Queen of Africa Dolls
https://queensofafricadolls.com

Rah Loves Boutique
https://www.rahlovesboutique.com

Shine Cloth
https://shinecloth.com

Stina & Mae
https://www.stinaandmae.com

Step Stitches
https://www.stepstitches.com

Swimma (Swimwear)
https://swimma.co.za/wp3

The Black Toy Store
https://blacktoystore.com

The Conscious Kid Book Subscription
https://www.theconsciouskid.org

The Fresh Dolls
https://thefreshdolls.com

The Rooted Baby
https://rootedbabyco.com

The Stork Bag
https://thestorkbag.com

Toys Like Me
https://toyslikeme.com

Trinity Designs
https://www.trinitydesignsinc.com

Uzuri Kid Kidz
https://www.uzurikidkidz.com

Yinibini Baby
https://www.yinibinibaby.com

Racial Justice Initiatives to Join & Support

A New Way of Life
http://anewwayoflife.org

Acta Non Verba: Youth Urban Farm Project
https://anvfarm.org/mission

Advancement Project
https://advancementproject.org/home

African American Farmers of California Demo Farm
africanamericanfarmersofca@gmail.com
Anti-Recidivism Coalition
1320 E. 7th Street Suite 260
Los Angeles, CA 90021
(213) 955-5885
https://antirecidivism.org

Black Farmers and Agriculturalists Association
https://www.bfaa4us.org

Blacks in Government
3005 Georgia Avenue, NW
Washington, DC 20001-3807
bignet.org

Black Lives Matter Movement
https://blacklivesmatter.com

BYP100
https://www.byp100.org

Center for Court Innovation
520 8th Avenue
18th Floor
New York, NY 10018
(646) 386-3100
https://www.courtinnovation.org

Center for Policing Equity
1925 Century Park East, #1700
Los Angeles, CA 90067
(347) 948-9953
https://policingequity.org

Center on Juvenile and Criminal Justice
424 Guerrero Street, Suite A

San Francisco, CA 94110
(415) 621-5661
http://www.cjcj.org

Circle for Justice Initiatives
https://www.cjifund.org

Coalition for Public Safety
https://www.coalitionforpublicsafety.org

Color of Food
https://thecolorofood.com

Conference of National Black Churches
678 Beckwith Street, Southwest
Atlanta, Georgia 30314-4108
(404) 688-6052
https://www.thecnbc.net

Congressional Black Caucus
https://cbc.house.gov

Ella Baker Center for Human Rights
1419 34th Avenue, Suite 202
Oakland, CA 94601
(510) 428-3939
https://ellabakercenter.org

Equal Justice Initiative
122 Commerce Street
Montgomery, AL 36104
(334) 269-1803
https://eji.org

Families Against Mandatory Minimums
1100 H Street NW, Suite 1000
Washington, D.C. 20005
(202) 822-6700
https://famm.org

Farms to Grow, Inc
https://www.farmstogrow.com

Federation of Southern Cooperatives/Land Assistance Fund
2769 Church Street
East Point, Georgia, 30344
(404) 765-0991

https://www.federation.coop

Leadership Conference Education Fund
L Street NW, Suite 1100
Washington, DC 20036
(202) 466-3311 1620
https://civilrights.org/edfund

Movement for Black Lives
https://m4bl.org

NAACP
https://www.naacp.org
NAACP Legal Fund, Inc
https://www.naacpldf.org

National Action Network
https://nationalactionnetwork.net

National African American Gun Association
https://naaga.co

National Bar Association
1816 12th Street NW
Washington, DC 20009
(202) 842-3900
https://nationalbar.org

National Black Church Initiative
P.O. Box 65177
Washington, DC 20035-1577
(202) 744-0184
https://www.naltblackchurch.com

National Black Contractors Association
6125 Imperial Avenue
San Diego, CA 92114
(619) 263-9791
https://www.nationalbca.org

National Black Famers Associations
68 Wind Road
Baskerville, VA 23915
(434) 676-6232
https://www.nationalblackfarmersassociation.org

National Black Food and Justice Alliance

https://www.blackfoodjustice.org

National Black Growers Council
https://nationalblackgrowerscouncil.com

National Organization of Black Law Enforcement Executives
4609-F Pinecrest Office Park Drive
Alexandria, VA 22312-1442
(703) 658-1529
https://noblenational.org

Prison Policy Initiative
https://www.prisonpolicy.org

Rainbow Push Coalition
https://rainbowpush.org

Rid-All Green Partnership (Black Farmers Advocacy)
https://www.greennghetto.org

Southern Center for Human Rights
60 Walton Street NW
Atlanta, GA 30303-2149
(404) 688-1202
https://www.schr.org

Southeastern African American Farmers Organic Network (Atlanta, GA)
http://saafon.org

Survived & Punished
https://survivedandpunished.org

The Marshall Project
156 West 56th Street, Suite 701
New York, NY 10019
(212) 803-5200
https://www.themarshallproject.org

The Sentencing Project
1705 DeSales Street, NW 8th Floor
Washington, D.C. 20036
(202) 628-0871
https://www.sentencingproject.org

The Tow Foundation
50 Locust Avenue, Suite 1
New Canaan, CT 06840-4737
(203) 761-6604
https://www.towfoundation.org

Urban Farming Institute of Boston
487 Norfolk Street
Mattapan, MA 02126
(617) 989-9920
http://www.urbanfarminginstitute.org

Urban Growers Collective
1200 W. 35th Street, Box 118
Chicago, IL 60609
(773) 376-8882
https://urbangrowerscollective.org

Vera Institute of Justice
34 35th Street
Suite 4-2A
Brooklyn, NY 11232
(212) 334-1300
https://www.vera.org

Voix Noire
https://voixnoire.com

Women's Prison Association
110 Second Avenue
New York, NY 10003
(646) 292-7740
https://www.wpaonline.org

Your Bountiful Harvest (Farm Consulting & Advocacy)
https://yourbountifulharvest.wixsite.com/yourbountifulharvest

Youth Build
58 Day St
Somerville, MA 02144
(617) 623-9900
https://www.youthbuild.org

BLACK LED LGBTQ+ ORGANIZATIONS & INITIATIVES

Anti-Violence Project
https://avp.org

Audre Lorde Project
https://alp.org

Black & Pink
https://resist.org/grantees/black-and-pink

Black AIDS Institute
https://blackaids.org

Black LGBTQIA + Migrant Project
https://transgenderlawcenter.org/programs/blmp

Black Trans Femmes in the Arts
https://www.artsbusinesscollaborative.org/asp-products/black-trans-femmes-in-the-arts-sponsored-projected

Black Trans Advocacy Coalition
https://blacktrans.org

Black Trans Travel Fund
https://www.blacktranstravelfund.com

Black Visions Collective
https://www.blackvisionsmn.org

Brave Space Alliance
https://www.bravespacealliance.org

Center for Black Equity
https://centerforblackequity.org

House of GG
https://houseofgg.org

Kween Culture Initiative
https://kweenculture.com

LGBTQ+ Freedom Fund
https://www.lgbtqfund.org

Marsha P. Johnson Institute
https://marshap.org

META Center, Inc.
https://metacenterinc.org

National Black Justice Coalition
http://nbjc.org

SNaPCo
https://www.lgbtqracialjusticefund.org/grantees/snapco

TGI Justice Project
http://www.tgijp.org

The Okra Project
https://www.theokraproject.com

The Transgender District
https://www.transgenderdistrictsf.com

Trans Women of Color Collective
https://www.twocc.us

Trans Justice Funding Project
https://www.transjusticefundingproject.org

Transgender Awareness Alliance
https://www.taagg.org

Youth Breakout
http://www.youthbreakout.org

DISCLAIMER: Before using financial services and investing always consult with a financial professional. Before using health products and services always consult with your doctor.

Questions? Comments? Please contact us:
Peculiar Capital LLC
info@peculiar-capital.com
www.peculiar-capital.com

Made in the USA
Middletown, DE
01 November 2023